D0187984

vegetarian

the perfect guide to meat-free meals

STEP-BY-STEP

vegetarian

the perfect guide to meat-free meals

STEP-BY-STEP

LOVE FOOD™

First published in 2013
LOVE FOOD is an imprint of Parragon Books Ltd

Parragon
Chartist House
15–17 Trim Street
Bath, BA1 1HA, UK

www.parragon.com/lovefood

ISBN: 978-1-4723-0725-5

Printed in China

Photography by Mike Cooper
Home economy by Lincoln Jefferson
Cover design by Geoff Borin; background texture from Getty Images
Internal design by Talking Design
Introduction by Christine McFadden
New recipes by Christine McFadden
Edited by Fiona Biggs

Notes for the Reader
This book uses both metric and imperial measurements. Follow the same units of measurement throughout; do not mix metric and imperial. All spoon measurements are level: teaspoons are assumed to be 5 ml, and tablespoons are assumed to be 15 ml. Unless otherwise stated, milk is assumed to be full fat, eggs and individual vegetables are medium, and pepper is freshly ground black pepper. Unless otherwise stated, all root vegetables should be washed in plain water and peeled prior to using.

Garnishes, decorations and serving suggestions are all optional and not necessarily included in the recipe ingredients or method. The times given are an approximate guide only. Preparation times differ according to the techniques used by different people and the cooking times may also vary from those given. Optional ingredients, variations or serving suggestions have not been included in the time calculations.

Recipes using raw or very lightly cooked eggs should be avoided by infants, the elderly, pregnant women, convalescents and anyone suffering from an illness. Pregnant and breastfeeding women are advised to avoid eating peanuts and peanut products. Sufferers from nut allergies should be aware that some of the ready-made ingredients used in the recipes in this book may contain nuts. Always check the packaging before use.

Vegetarians should be aware that some of the ready-made ingredients used in the recipes in this book may contain animal products. Always check the packaging before use.

contents

introduction

This book will introduce you to the delights of vegetarian cooking today – which is exciting, colourful and tasty. It includes easy to follow and irresistible meat-free recipes that will appeal to carnivores and vegetarians alike. So, whether you want to switch to a wholly vegetarian diet, or to increase the vegetarian element in a mixed diet, this book offers delicious and fail-safe recipes to guarantee success every time.

why you need this book

Although cooking for a vegetarian diet isn't necessarily any more difficult than for a mixed diet, there are certain issues to be aware of, especially for people new to this. For example, it's important to ensure you are eating a balanced diet and are aware of the non-vegetarian ingredients that may be hidden in ready-made foods. It's also essential to offer a variety of dishes and the 60 recipes in this book include many exciting and less-familiar options to tempt even reluctant vegetable eaters.

the everyday vegetarian

If you're switching to a vegetarian diet, make the change gradually. Start by introducing a vegetarian dish to your normal diet once or twice a week, then eliminate red meat one month, poultry the next, and finally fish. That way your digestive system will have time to adjust.

Even if you don't intend to make a complete change, you can gradually include more vegetarian foods on the menu. Try starting a meal with a colourful salad (see chapter 2) or serve grains or pulses as an alternative to potatoes as an accompaniment. Don't be timid with herbs. A generous shower adds colour and freshness to a dish, as well as extra vitamins.

To tempt reluctant vegetable eaters, whether adults or children, go for mildly flavoured and easily chewed varieties such as peas, green beans and sweetcorn. Go easy on Brussels sprouts and cabbage. Disguised with a tasty sauce, crisp crumbs or melted cheese, bite-sized chunks of less popular vegetables such

as cauliflower or broccoli usually go down a treat. Sweet and sticky roasted root vegetables are popular too. The trick is to keep the portions small, avoid vegetables with strong smells and to make the dish look appetizing.

Another way of getting more vegetables into the diet is to purée them and serve as bright, fresh-tasting soups with appetizing garnishes (see chapter 1). Starchy vegetables such as carrots and broad beans also make lovely dips.

catering for both vegetarians and non-vegetarians

Creating a balanced and satisfying meal for both vegetarians and meat-eaters needn't mean extra work for the cook or a compromise over what is served. There is no need to cook something different for the vegetarians, and the same meal can be shared with family or friends. For example, begin cooking the dish with ingredients that are common to both diets, such as a sauce of fried onions, peppers and tomatoes. The mixture can then be divided and one part finished with meat or fish, and the other with a vegetarian protein food such as tofu, beans or cheese.

This approach can be applied to some of the recipes in this book. For example, the mushrooms in Watercress & Mushroom Pâté (page 54) could be replaced with chicken livers. Or you could divide the Chickpea, Aubergine & Red Pepper Casserole (page 180) and simmer some cubed lamb in the meat-eaters' portion.

balancing your diet

The general principles of a balanced diet are the same for vegetarians as for meat-eaters: eat a variety of foods, including plenty of whole grains, pulses, vegetables and fruit, moderate amounts of protein foods, and small amounts of fat, salt and sugar. With today's hectic life-style, diet balancing usually involves juggling what you know you should eat with what can practically be achieved and, just as important, what you enjoy. You don't necessarily have to eat nutritionally balanced meals every day, but you should aim to do so over several days.

essential nutrients for vegetarians

As with any restricted diet, it's good to have some basic nutritional knowledge to help maintain good health. You'll need alternative sources of important nutrients normally supplied by meat and fish: iron, B vitamins and protein, for example.

> **Carbohydrates:** There are two basic types: complex starches which provide slow-release energy that stabilizes blood-sugar, and simple sugars which provide fast-release energy.

Good sources of complex starches: Bread, pasta, rice, oats, couscous, quinoa, pulses, potatoes, yams and other root vegetables.
Good sources of simple sugars: Fruits, fruit juices, vegetables, milk and table sugar.

> **Fat:** Fat is a concentrated source of energy and supplies essential fatty acids needed for brain

function and normal growth. Vegans, particularly children, need energy-dense foods to help reduce the bulk of a carbohydrate-based diet. All fats and oils contain two types of fatty acids: saturated fats tend to be solid at room temperature and unsaturated fats are usually liquid. They can help lower blood cholesterol.

Good sources of saturated fatty acids: Eggs, full-fat dairy foods, coconut oil, palm oil.

Good sources of unsaturated fatty acids: Avocados, eggs, leafy vegetables, peanut butter, tahini, vegetable margarine, olives, nuts and seeds, vegetable, nut and seed oils.

> **Protein:** Protein is made up of amino acids vital for growth, maintenance and repair of the body. Some of the essential amino acids that make up 'complete' protein in animal foods are missing from plant foods. It's easy, however, for vegetarians to get the right amount as long as you eat combinations of plant proteins. An example is a grain with a pulse, as in baked beans on toast, or rice and lentils.

Good sources of protein: Dairy products, eggs, beans (particularly soya beans and soya products such as tofu), chick-peas, lentils, rice, quinoa, nuts, seeds, sea vegetables.

> **Vitamins:** Vitamins are vital for good health. Provided you eat a variety of fruits, vegetables, nuts, pulses and grains, you should get all that you need. Vegans need plant-based sources of vitamin D, and usually a B12 supplement to replace that found in meat and eggs.

Good sources of vitamin D: Eggs, vegetable margarine, dairy products, fortified breakfast cereals, soya milk. The body also manufactures its own vitamin D when the skin is exposed to sunlight.

Good sources of Vitamin B12: Eggs, cheese, yogurt, vegetable margarine, milk, yeast extract, some fortified breakfast cereals.

> **Minerals:** Minerals are as important as vitamins. They come from a range of different foods, so a varied diet is essential. Calcium and iron are particularly important for women.

Good sources of calcium: Dairy products, nuts, seeds, tofu, fortified flour, citrus fruits, green vegetables, sea vegetables.

Good sources of iron: Egg yolk, pulses, dried apricots, spinach, watercress, molasses, chocolate.

substituting foods

When you switch to a vegetarian diet, you'll need alternatives to ingredients made with animal foods.

	substitute
Chicken and meat stock	Home-made vegetable stock or vegetable bouillon powder
Eggs	Tofu
Gelatin	Agar-agar, arrowroot, carrageen, kudzu powder
Lard	Vegetable fat
Margarine	Vegetable margarine
Marmite	Yeast extract
Milk	Nut milk, rice milk, soya milk
Suet	Vegetable suet

hidden ingredients

When buying processed foods, check the labels for non-vegetarian/vegan ingredients. In most cases, you'll be able to find a suitable alternative, such as vegetarian Cheddar cheese.

	where found
Anchovies, fermented fish	Worcestershire sauce, fish sauce
Animal fats (butter, suet, lard)	Biscuits, cakes, margarine, ready-made pastry
Eggs	Biscuits, cakes, sauces
Rennet (from calves)	Cheese

storecupboard standbys

It's worth stocking up with not just the basics but also the more unusual items, such as colourful pulses, different types of rice and interesting spices. That way you'll always be able to rustle up tasty meals with whatever you have to hand.

Oils : olive, rapeseed, groundnut
Vinegars : cider, red wine, thick balsamic
Dried herbs : oregano, rosemary, sage, thyme
Grains : barley, bulgur wheat, couscous, polenta, basmati rice, jasmine rice, red rice
Pasta : shapes and ribbons
Noodles : cellophane, egg, rice, soba, udon
Dried pulses : beans, chickpeas and lentils
Nuts : almonds, cashews, hazelnuts, peanuts, walnuts
Dried fruit : apricots, pears, prunes
Sea vegetables : arame, hiziki, nori
Seeds : pumpkin, sunflower, sesame
Sauces, pastes and condiments : harissa sauce, miso, mustards, sea salt flakes, soy sauce, tahini, tomato purée, wasabi
Spices : black peppercorns, chilli powder, cumin, coriander, nutmeg, paprika, turmeric
Canned and bottled foods : coconut milk, pulses, tomatoes, olives
Stock : vegetable bouillon powder

sourcing specialist ingredients

Good hunting grounds are Asian and African grocery stores. The better health-food shops are worth a visit too. Even more rewarding is the internet. Here you can find specialist suppliers of every imaginable ingredient, from exotic spices and heirloom pulses, to top-notch oils, grains and flour.

tips and techniques

Preparing vegetarian meals can take a bit more time than meat-based meals, but there are ways of making meal preparation easier and saving time without cutting corners.

make the most of the freezer

> It's well worth cooking dishes in bulk and freezing portions for later on. This will give you a store of pre-cooked dishes ready for when you're too busy to cook or unexpected guests arrive.
> Soak and cook dried pulses, then freeze in portions ready for adding to stews and soups.
> Make the most of seasonal fresh produce. Buy fruit and vegetables in bulk when they are at their best and cheapest. Freeze on the day of purchase.

use a pressure cooker

> Use the pressure cooker to cook soups, stocks, dried beans, chickpeas, and dense-fleshed vegetables in a fraction of the normal time.
> You'll save valuable nutrients as the cooking water isn't lost.
> Vegetables keep their natural bright colour as they are not exposed to oxygen in the air.

use a slow cooker

> A slow cooker is ideal for cooking healthy vegetarian meals. You need very little fat as the food doesn't need an initial frying.
> The meal can be left to gently simmer for hours, ready to serve when it suits you.
> You can serve people at different times without having to reheat the food. For example, young children can be served first, then you can add more spices and seasoning to the adult portions and serve later on.

soups & starters

sweet potato & apple soup

serves 6

ingredients

1 tbsp butter
3 leeks, thinly sliced
1 large carrot, thinly sliced
600 g/1 lb 5 oz sweet
  potatoes, peeled and
  diced

2 large Bramley apples,
  peeled, cored and diced
1.2 litres/2 pints water
freshly grated nutmeg
225 ml/8 fl oz apple juice

225 ml/8 fl oz single cream
salt and pepper
snipped fresh chives or
  coriander, to garnish

>1 Melt the butter in a large saucepan over a medium–low heat.

>2 Add the leeks, cover and cook for 6–8 minutes, or until soft, stirring frequently.

>3 Add the carrot, sweet potatoes, apples and water. Lightly season to taste with salt, pepper and nutmeg. Bring to the boil, reduce the heat and simmer, covered, for about 20 minutes, stirring occasionally, until the vegetables are very tender.

>4 Leave the soup to cool slightly, then purée in the pan with a hand-held blender.

>5 Stir in the apple juice, place over a low heat and simmer for about 10 minutes, until heated through.

>6 Stir in the cream and simmer for a further 5 minutes, stirring frequently, until heated through. Taste and adjust the seasoning, if necessary.

Ladle the soup into warmed bowls, garnish with chives and serve.

roasted root soup with ginger & crème fraîche

serves 4–6

ingredients

1 onion
½ small swede
1 sweet potato
2 carrots
1 potato

5 tbsp olive oil
2 tbsp tomato purée
¼ tsp pepper
2 large garlic cloves, peeled
2 tbsp groundnut oil

2 x 5-cm/2-inch pieces
fresh ginger, sliced into
thin shreds
850 ml/1½ pints hot
vegetable stock

½ tsp sea salt
crème fraîche and
roughly chopped
fresh flat-leaf parsley,
to garnish

>1 Preheat the oven to 190°C/375°F/ Gas Mark 5. Peel the vegetables and cut into large, even-sized chunks.

>2 Mix the olive oil, tomato purée and pepper in a large bowl. Add the vegetables and the garlic and toss to coat.

>3 Spread out the vegetables in a roasting tray. Roast in the preheated oven for 20 minutes, or until the garlic is soft. Remove the garlic and set aside. Roast the vegetables for a further 10–15 minutes, until tender.

>4 Meanwhile, heat the groundnut oil in a frying pan over a high heat. Add the ginger and fry, turning constantly, for 1–2 minutes, until crisp.

23

>5 Immediately remove the ginger from the pan and drain on kitchen paper. Set aside and keep warm.

>6 Put the garlic and the other roasted vegetables into a food processor. Process in short bursts to a rough-textured purée.

>7 Pour the purée into a saucepan and add the stock. Add the salt, then simmer, stirring, for 1–2 minutes, until heated through.

>8 Ladle the soup into warmed serving bowls and swirl in a little crème fraîche.

Top with the sizzled ginger threads and
chopped parsley and serve immediately.

chilled garlic soup

serves 4–6

ingredients

500 g/1 lb 2 oz day-old
 country-style white bread,
 crusts removed and torn
5 large garlic cloves, halved
125 ml/4 fl oz extra virgin
 olive oil, plus a little extra
 for drizzling
4–5 tbsp sherry vinegar
300 g/10½ oz ground
 almonds
1.2 litres/2 pints chilled water
salt and white pepper
seedless white grapes,
 to garnish

> **>1** Put the bread in a bowl with just enough cold water to cover and leave to soak for 15 minutes.

> **>2** Squeeze the bread dry and transfer to a food processor.

To serve, ladle into bowls, float the halved grapes on top and drizzle with oil.

>3 Add the garlic, oil, vinegar to taste, the ground almonds and 250 ml/9 fl oz of the chilled water to the food processor and process until blended.

>4 With the motor running, slowly pour in the remaining water until a smooth soup forms. Taste and add extra vinegar if necessary. Cover and chill for at least 4 hours, then stir well and adjust the seasoning if necessary.

yellow tomato gazpacho

serves 4–6

ingredients

900 g/2 lb large yellow
tomatoes, halved
½ cucumber, peeled,
deseeded and diced
1 yellow pepper, deseeded
and diced

100 g/3½ oz red cherry
tomatoes, deseeded and
chopped
3 large spring onions,
finely chopped
1–2 green chillies, deseeded
and finely chopped

2 tbsp wine vinegar
3 tbsp extra virgin olive oil,
plus extra for drizzling
4 garlic cloves
½ tbsp sea salt flakes,
plus extra to taste

¼ tsp pepper, plus extra
to taste
¼ tsp sugar
small handful basil leaves,
shredded, to garnish
garlic croûtons, to serve

>1 Scoop out the seeds and juice from the yellow tomatoes.

>2 Pass the seeds and juice through a sieve set over a bowl. Chop the flesh and add to the bowl.

>3 Set aside 4 tablespoons each of the cucumber and yellow pepper. Set aside all of the chopped cherry tomatoes

>4 Add the remaining cucumber and yellow pepper to the yellow tomatoes. Add the onions, chilli, vinegar and oil.

>5 Tip into a food processor. Process, scraping down frequently, for 2 minutes, until very smooth. Pour back into the bowl.

>6 Put the garlic into a mortar with the salt and crush with a pestle. Stir into the tomato mixture with the pepper and sugar. Chill for several hours until really cold.

>7 Check the seasoning, adding more salt and pepper as necessary. Ladle into chilled soup plates or bowls.

>8 Top with the reserved yellow pepper, the cucumber and the cherry tomatoes.

Add a slick of oil and a few shredded basil leaves and serve with garlic croûtons.

jerusalem artichoke soup

serves 4–6

ingredients

55 g/2 oz butter
2 onions, chopped
675 g/1 lb 8 oz Jerusalem
 artichokes, peeled, sliced
 and dropped into water to
 prevent discolouration

850 ml/1½ pints vegetable
 stock
300 ml/10 fl oz milk
salt and pepper

croûtons

4 tbsp vegetable oil
2 slices of day-old white
 bread, crusts removed,
 bread cut into 1-cm/
 ½-inch cubes

>1 To make the croûtons, heat the oil in a frying pan over a medium heat. Add the croûtons in a single layer and fry, tossing occasionally, until golden brown and crisp.

>2 Remove the pan from the heat and transfer the croûtons to kitchen paper to drain.

>3 Melt the butter in a large saucepan over a medium heat. Add the onions and cook until soft.

>4 Add the drained artichokes and mix well with the butter. Cover the pan and cook slowly over a low heat for about 10 minutes.

>5 Pour in the stock, bring to the boil, then reduce the heat and simmer, covered, for 20 minutes.

>6 Remove from the heat and blend in the saucepan using a hand-held blender. Stir in the milk, season to taste with salt and pepper, then return the soup to the heat and heat until hot.

Ladle the soup into warmed bowls, sprinkle over the croûtons and serve immediately.

leek & spinach soup

serves 4

ingredients
25 g/1 oz butter
2 leeks, trimmed, halved
lengthways and thinly
sliced
225 g/8 oz potatoes, cut
into bite-sized chunks
300 g/10½ oz spinach, stalks
discarded, leaves sliced
300 ml/10 fl oz hot
vegetable stock
1 tsp lemon juice
pinch of freshly grated
nutmeg
sea salt and pepper
soured cream, to serve

>1 Melt the butter in a large saucepan
over a medium–low heat. Add the leeks
and potatoes, cover and gently cook for
10 minutes, or until beginning to soften.

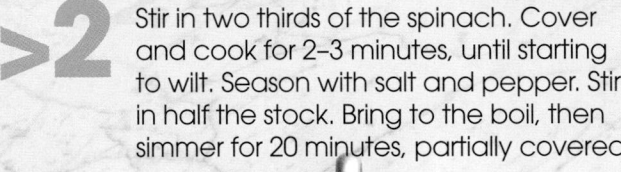

>2 Stir in two thirds of the spinach. Cover
and cook for 2–3 minutes, until starting
to wilt. Season with salt and pepper. Stir
in half the stock. Bring to the boil, then
simmer for 20 minutes, partially covered.

Ladle into bowls, swirl in a spoonful of soured cream and serve immediately.

>3 Transfer half the soup to a food processor and process until smooth. Return to the pan.

>4 Purée the remaining uncooked spinach and stock. Add to the soup in the pan. Stir in the lemon juice and nutmeg and gently reheat.

celeriac soup with cheese pastry sticks

serves 4

ingredients

3 tbsp olive oil
1 onion, chopped
1 celeriac, peeled and cut
 into chunks
1 litre/1¾ pints vegetable
 stock

1 small bunch fresh thyme,
 chopped
salt and pepper
fresh thyme sprigs, to garnish

cheese sticks

375 g/13 oz ready-made
 puff pastry, thawed if
 frozen
plain flour, for dusting
1 egg, beaten

100 g/3½ oz finely grated
 vegetarian Parmesan-
 style cheese
butter, for greasing
pepper

> 1 Heat the oil in a large saucepan over a medium heat, add the onion and cook, stirring frequently, for 4–5 minutes, until soft but not coloured.

> 2 Add the celeriac and cook, stirring frequently, for 3–4 minutes. Pour in the stock and add the thyme. Simmer for 25 minutes, or until the celeriac is tender. Meanwhile, preheat the oven to 200°C/400°F/ Gas Mark 6.

> 3 To make the cheese sticks, thinly roll out the pastry on a floured work surface. Brush with half the egg, scatter over half the cheese and season well with pepper.

> 4 Fold the pastry in half. Brush with the remaining egg, scatter with the remaining cheese and season with pepper. Lightly grease and line two baking sheets.

39

>5 Cut the pastry into strips about 1 cm/
½ inch wide. Twist gently along their length
to produce spirals. Place on the prepared
baking sheets and bake in the preheated
oven for 5 minutes, or until crisp and golden.

>6 Purée the soup in the pan using a hand-held
blender and gently reheat. Season to taste
with salt and pepper.

Ladle the soup into warmed bowls, garnish with thyme sprigs and serve with the warm pastry sticks.

roast squash soup with cheese toasties

serves 4

ingredients

1 kg/2 lb 4 oz butternut
  squash, cut into small
  chunks
2 onions, cut into wedges
2 tbsp olive oil
2 garlic cloves, crushed
3–4 fresh thyme sprigs,
  leaves removed
1 litre/1¾ pints vegetable
  stock
150 ml/5 fl oz crème fraîche
salt and pepper
snipped fresh chives,
  to garnish

cheese toasties

1 baguette, thinly sliced
  diagonally
40 g/1½ oz vegetarian hard
  cheese, grated

>1 Preheat the oven to 190°C/375°F/Gas Mark
5. Place the squash, onions, oil, garlic and
thyme in a roasting tin. Toss together and
spread out in a single layer. Roast in the
preheated oven for 50–60 minutes, stirring
occasionally, until the vegetables are
tender and caramelized in places.

>2 Transfer the vegetables to a saucepan.
Add half the stock and purée with a
hand-held blender until smooth. Stir in the
remaining stock and crème fraîche. Season
to taste with salt and pepper, and heat
through gently.

Serve immediately with the cheese
toasties on the side.

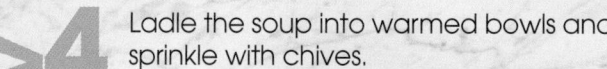

>**3** To make the toasties, preheat the grill to
high. Toast the sliced baguette under the
preheated grill for 1–2 minutes on each side
until pale golden in colour. Sprinkle with the
cheese and return to the grill for a further
30–40 seconds, until melted and bubbling.

>**4** Ladle the soup into warmed bowls and
sprinkle with chives.

blue cheese & herb pâté

serves 4

ingredients
150 g/5½ oz vegetarian
 low-fat soft cheese
350 g/12 oz fromage frais
115 g/4 oz vegetarian blue
 cheese, crumbled
55 g/2 oz dried cranberries,
 finely chopped
5 tbsp chopped fresh herbs,
 such as parsley, chives, dill
 and tarragon
85 g/3 oz butter
2 tbsp chopped walnuts
granary toast or bread
 sticks, to serve

>1 Beat the soft cheese to soften, then gradually beat in the fromage frais until smooth. Add the blue cheese, cranberries and herbs and stir together. Spoon the mixture into four 150-ml/5-fl oz ramekins and carefully smooth the tops.

>2 Clarify the butter by gently heating it in a small saucepan until melted. Skim any foam off the surface and discard.

44

Serve the pâté in the ramekins with granary toast on the side.

Carefully pour the clear yellow top layer into a small jug, discarding the milky liquid left in the pan.

Pour a little of the clarified butter over the top of each pâté and sprinkle with the walnuts. Chill for at least 30 minutes until firm.

grilled aubergines with red pepper, feta & mint

serves 4

ingredients

1 red pepper, halved and deseeded

2 large firm aubergines, sliced crossways into 2-cm/¾-inch slices

olive oil, for brushing

2 garlic cloves, crushed

juice of 1 lemon

1½ tsp cumin seeds, crushed

50 g/1¾ oz vegetarian feta cheese, crumbled

2 tbsp roughly chopped fresh mint leaves

sea salt flakes and pepper

>1 Preheat the grill to high. Put the red pepper halves cut-side down on a roasting tray. Place under a very hot grill for about 10 minutes, or until the skin is black and blistered.

>2 Remove from the heat and cover with a clean tea towel. Leave for 10 minutes to loosen the skin. Peel off the skin and cut the flesh into 5-mm/¼-inch dice.

>3 Preheat a ridged griddle pan over a high heat. Brush the aubergine slices with oil on both sides and place in the pan, in batches, if necessary. Cook for about 2 minutes on each side, until grill marks appear.

>4 Carefully remove the aubergine slices from the pan. Cut the larger slices in half.

>5 In a large bowl, combine the garlic, red pepper, lemon juice and cumin. Season with salt and pepper.

>6 Add the aubergine slices, turning carefully to coat, then arrange on a serving platter.

48

Scatter over the cheese and mint leaves and serve at room temperature.

vegetable & black bean spring rolls

serves 4

ingredients

2 tbsp groundnut oil or vegetable oil, plus extra for deep-frying

4 spring onions, cut into 5-cm/2-inch lengths and shredded lengthways

2.5-cm/1-inch piece fresh ginger, peeled and finely chopped

1 large carrot, peeled and cut into matchsticks

1 red pepper, deseeded and cut into matchsticks

6 tbsp black bean sauce

55 g/2 oz fresh beansprouts

200 g/7 oz canned water chestnuts, drained and roughly chopped

5-cm/2-inch piece cucumber, cut into matchsticks

8 x 20-cm/8-inch square spring roll wrappers

sweet chilli dipping sauce, to serve (optional)

>1 Heat 2 tablespoons of the oil in a preheated wok, add the spring onions, ginger, carrot and red pepper and stir-fry over a medium–high heat for 2–3 minutes.

>2 Add the black bean sauce, beansprouts, water chestnuts and cucumber and stir-fry for 1–2 minutes. Leave to cool.

>3 Remove the spring roll wrappers from the packet, keeping them in a pile, covered with clingfilm, to prevent them drying out. Lay one wrapper on a work surface in front of you in a diamond shape and brush the edges with water. Put a spoonful of the filling near one corner and fold the corner over the filling.

>4 Roll over again and then fold the side corners over the filling.

>5 Roll up to seal the filling completely. Repeat with the remaining wrappers and filling.

>6 Heat the oil in a clean wok to 180–190°C/350–375°F, or until a cube of bread browns in 30 seconds. Add the rolls, in 2–3 batches, and cook for 2–3 minutes, until crisp and golden all over. Remove with a slotted spoon, drain on kitchen paper and keep warm while you cook the remaining rolls.

Serve the rolls hot with the sweet chilli dipping
sauce on the side, if using.

watercress & mushroom pâté

serves 3–4

ingredients

25 g/1 oz butter
3 large spring onions,
  chopped
1 tsp coriander seeds,
  crushed
85 g/3 oz flat mushrooms,
  chopped
100 g/3½ oz trimmed
  watercress
100 g/3½ oz vegetarian
  curd cheese
a few drops of hot
  pepper sauce
sea salt and pepper
toast or crackers, to serve

> **1** Melt the butter in a frying pan over a medium–low heat, until sizzling. Add the spring onions and coriander seeds and gently fry for 5 minutes, until the onions are soft but not coloured.

> **2** Increase the heat to medium–high. Add the mushrooms and stir for 2 minutes, until the juices start to flow. Add the watercress and quickly cook until just wilted. Season with salt and pepper. Remove from the heat and leave to cool for a few minutes.

Serve straight from the bowl with toast.

> **>3** Tip the mixture into a food processor. Add the cheese and hot pepper sauce.

> **>4** Process to a smooth purée, scrape into a serving bowl, then cover and chill for 1 hour.

crumbed fennel fritters with spiced pepper mayo

serves 6

ingredients

3 fennel bulbs, trimmed
100 g/3½ oz stale white
   breadcrumbs
100 g/3½ oz vegetarian
   Parmesan-style cheese,
   finely grated

2 tsp fennel seeds (optional)
1 egg, beaten
sunflower oil, for frying
salt and pepper
lemon wedges, to serve

spiced pepper mayo

2 red peppers
1 egg
1 tsp Dijon mustard
2–3 tbsp white wine vinegar
pinch of salt

300 ml/10 fl oz sunflower
   oil
2 red chillies, deseeded
   and chopped
pepper

> **1** To make the mayo, preheat the oven to 220°C/425°F/Gas Mark 7. Put the red peppers on a baking sheet and cook in the preheated oven, turning frequently, for 10–15 minutes, or until blackened all over.

> **2** Put the peppers in a polythene bag, seal and leave to cool. Peel off the charred skins and remove the seeds.

> **3** Put the egg, mustard, vinegar and salt into a blender and process to combine. With the motor running, slowly trickle in about one third of the oil. Once the mixture starts to thicken, add the remaining oil more quickly.

> **4** When all the oil is incorporated, add the chillies and roasted peppers and process until smooth. Stir in a good grinding of pepper, then transfer to a serving dish, cover and refrigerate until required.

> 5 Bring a large saucepan of lightly salted water to the boil, add the fennel bulbs, bring back to the boil and cook for 15 minutes, or until almost tender. Drain and leave to cool, then carefully slice.

> 6 Mix the breadcrumbs and cheese together, stir in the fennel seeds, if using, and season to taste with salt and pepper.

> 7 Transfer the breadcrumb mixture to a large plate. Put the egg in a shallow dish. Coat the fennel slices in the egg and press the breadcrumb mixture firmly on to both sides of each slice.

> 8 Cover the base of a large frying pan with oil to a depth of about 1 cm/ ½ inch. Heat over a medium heat, add the fennel slices (in batches if necessary) and cook, turning once, until golden brown. Remove and drain on kitchen paper.

Serve immediately with lemon wedges for squeezing over and the mayo on the side.

grilled vegetable filo tarts

serves 6

ingredients

hazelnut oil or olive oil, for
  brushing
4 large sheets of filo pastry
1 small aubergine, sliced
  into 2-cm/¾-inch rounds

18 cherry tomatoes
1 large red pepper, halved
  and deseeded
1 tbsp capers

6 Kalamata olives, pitted
  and sliced
a few basil leaves, shredded
sea salt flakes and pepper

60

>1 Preheat the oven to 160°C/325°F/Gas Mark 3. Lightly oil six fluted metal tartlet tins.

>2 Cut the filo pastry into twenty-four 13-cm/ 5-inch squares. Cover with a clean damp cloth. Lightly brush 4 squares with oil. Sprinkle with a tiny pinch of salt.

>3 Stack the squares on top of each other, rotating so that the corners are offset like the petals of a flower.

>4 Place the stack in a tartlet tin, pressing well into the edge. Repeat with the remaining squares.

 **5** Bake in the preheated oven for 7–8 minutes, until golden. Remove from the oven and keep warm. Preheat the grill to high.

 **6** Place the aubergine, tomatoes and red pepper cut-side down on a roasting tray. Lightly brush the aubergine slices with oil. Place under the preheated grill for 10–12 minutes, or until the red pepper and tomatoes are slightly blackened and the aubergine is golden.

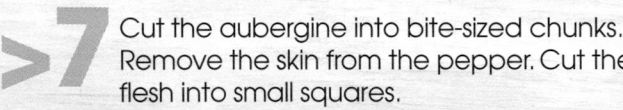 **7** Cut the aubergine into bite-sized chunks. Remove the skin from the pepper. Cut the flesh into small squares.

8 Carefully remove the pastry cases from the tins and fill with the vegetables. Lightly season with salt and pepper.

Scatter over the capers, olives and basil and serve warm.

bruschetta with broad beans, mint & goat's cheese

serves 6

ingredients

600 g/1 lb 5 oz shelled small
  broad beans (about 2.5
  kg/5 lb 8 oz unshelled
  weight)
3 tbsp extra virgin olive oil,
  plus extra for drizzling

1 tbsp lemon juice
1 tbsp chopped fresh mint
  leaves
6 slices ciabatta
1 large garlic clove, halved

6 tbsp soft fresh vegetarian
  goat's cheese
sea salt flakes and pepper

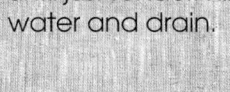

>1 Bring a large saucepan of lightly salted water to the boil. Add the beans, bring back to the boil and cook for 3 minutes, until just tender. Rinse under cold running water and drain.

>2 Slip off the bean skins and discard.

>3 Toss the beans with the oil, lemon juice and most of the mint. Season with a little salt and pepper.

>4 Tip the bean mixture into a food processor. Process briefly to a chunky purée.

>5 Toast the bread on both sides. While the bread is still warm, rub one side of each slice with the cut garlic clove. Drizzle with oil.

>6 Cut each bread slice in half. Spread with the bean mixture and top with a little goat's cheese.

Sprinkle with the remaining mint and serve
immediately.

salads & light meals

pear, celery, blue cheese & walnut salad

serves 4

ingredients

4 celery sticks
1 large, juicy red-skinned
  pear
lemon juice
3 tbsp chopped fresh
  flat-leaf parsley

150 g/5½ oz dark green
  salad leaves, such as
  rocket, watercress or baby
  spinach
100 g/3½ oz vegetarian
  blue cheese, broken into
  small chunks

4 tbsp roughly chopped
  walnuts
sea salt flakes

dressing

1 large, juicy pear
1 tbsp lemon juice
4 tbsp walnut oil
¼ tsp pepper
sea salt flakes

>1 Trim the celery and remove the strings with a swivel peeler. Slice into bite-sized pieces. Put into a shallow bowl.

>2 Quarter and core the pear but do not peel. Slice each quarter lengthways into thin segments. Add to the celery. Sprinkle with a little lemon juice to prevent discoloration.

>3 To make the dressing, quarter and core the pear. Slice one quarter lengthways into thin segments. Add to the pears in the bowl. Peel and roughly chop the remaining pear quarters.

>4 Process the chopped pear with the remaining dressing ingredients with a hand-held blender. Process for 30 seconds until very smooth. Scrape into a small bowl.

71

>5 Toss the celery and pears with about 5 tablespoons of the dressing, or enough to just coat. Stir in the parsley. Season with a pinch of salt.

>6 Arrange the salad leaves on individual plates. Pile the pear and celery mixture attractively on top. Sprinkle with the cheese and nuts.

Spoon the remaining dressing over the salad and serve immediately.

watercress, courgette & mint salad

serves 4

ingredients
2 courgettes, cut into
  batons
100 g/3½ oz French beans,
  cut into thirds
1 green pepper, deseeded
  and cut into strips
2 celery sticks, sliced
1 bunch watercress
salt

dressing
200 ml/7 fl oz natural yogurt
1 garlic clove, crushed
2 tbsp chopped fresh mint
pepper

> **1** Bring a saucepan of lightly salted water to the boil, add the courgette batons and beans, bring back to the boil and cook for 7–8 minutes.

> **2** Drain, rinse under cold running water and drain again. Set aside to cool completely.

Spoon the dressing over the salad and serve immediately.

>3 Mix the courgettes and beans with the green pepper strips, celery and watercress in a large serving bowl.

>4 To make the dressing, combine the yogurt, garlic and mint in a small bowl. Season to taste with pepper.

carrot, coconut & mango salad

serves 2–3

ingredients

350 g/12 oz young carrots, scrubbed

1 ripe mango, about 375 g/13 oz, peeled and cut into small cubes

55 g/2 oz fresh coconut flesh, very thinly sliced

3 tbsp chopped fresh coriander

3 tbsp toasted skinned hazelnuts, roughly chopped

½ tsp muscovado sugar

½ tsp sea salt flakes

finely grated rind of 1 lime

lime segments, to garnish

dressing

1 tsp muscovado sugar

¼ tsp sea salt

juice of 1 lime

¼–½ small green chilli, deseeded and very finely chopped

3 tbsp hazelnut oil or light olive oil

pepper

>1 Cut the carrots into 5-cm/2-inch lengths. Using a swivel peeler, shave into wide ribbons, discarding the woody core. Put into a shallow dish and add the mango and coconut.

>2 To make the dressing, dissolve the sugar and salt in the lime juice. Stir in the chilli and add pepper to taste. Add the oil and whisk until smooth.

>3 Pour the dressing over the carrot mixture, tossing well. Leave to stand at room temperature for 20 minutes to allow the flavours to develop.

>4 Add the coriander and toss again.

77

>5 Mix the hazelnuts with the sugar, salt and lime rind.

>6 Arrange the carrot mixture on individual serving plates and sprinkle with the nut mixture.

Garnish with lime segments and serve.

warm red lentil salad with goat's cheese

serves 4

ingredients

2 tbsp olive oil
2 tsp cumin seeds
2 garlic cloves, crushed
2 tsp grated fresh ginger
300 g/10½ oz red split lentils

700 ml/1¼ pints vegetable
   stock
2 tbsp chopped fresh mint
2 tbsp chopped fresh
   coriander

2 red onions, thinly sliced
200 g/7 oz baby spinach
   leaves
1 tsp hazelnut oil
150 g/5½ oz vegetarian soft
   goat's cheese

4 tbsp Greek-style yogurt
pepper
lemon wedges, to garnish
rye bread, to serve

>1 Heat half the olive oil in a large saucepan over a medium heat. Add the cumin seeds, garlic and ginger and cook, stirring constantly, for 2 minutes.

>2 Stir in the lentils and return to the heat. Add the stock, a ladleful at a time, until it is all absorbed, stirring constantly – this will take about 20 minutes. Remove from the heat and stir in the herbs.

>3 Meanwhile, heat the remaining olive oil in a frying pan over a medium heat. Add the onions and cook, stirring frequently, for 10 minutes, or until soft and lightly browned.

>4 Put the spinach into a bowl, pour over the hazelnut oil and toss well. Divide between individual serving plates.

>5 Mash the cheese with the yogurt in a small bowl and season to taste with pepper.

>6 Divide the lentils between the plates and top with the onions and the goat's cheese mixture.

Garnish with lemon wedges and serve with
rye bread.

spring cabbage & radish slaw with pumpkin seeds

serves 4–6

ingredients

1 Hispi spring cabbage, or
¼ head white cabbage
10–15 radishes, trimmed and
  sliced
½ small red onion, thinly sliced
3 tbsp pumpkin seeds
small bunch dill, about 20 g/
  ¾ oz, thick stems removed,
  leaves roughly sliced
2 small handfuls micro-leaves,
  such as radish sprouts
1 handful pea shoots
salt

dressing

3 tbsp Greek-style yogurt
1 tbsp whipping cream
2 tsp extra virgin olive oil
¾ tsp Dijon mustard
good squeeze of lemon juice

>1 Discard any coarse outer leaves from the cabbage. Trim the base and cut the cabbage in quarters lengthways. Cut out the core and discard. Slice each quarter crossways into ribbons. Place in a colander set over a bowl and sprinkle with salt. Toss with your hands and leave to stand for 30 minutes.

>2 To make the dressing, combine all the ingredients in a small bowl, mixing well.

Scatter the micro-leaves and pea shoots over the top of the slaw and serve.

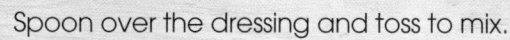

>**3** Blot the cabbage with kitchen paper. Tip into a shallow serving dish. Add the radishes, onion, pumpkin seeds and dill.

>**4** Spoon over the dressing and toss to mix.

borlotti bean, tomato & onion salad with eggs

serves 4

ingredients

250 g/9 oz dried borlotti
  beans, soaked in cold
  water for several hours
2 large garlic cloves,
  crushed
juice of 2 lemons
6 tbsp extra virgin olive oil

1 tsp salt
1 small onion, finely diced
2 tomatoes, deseeded and
  finely diced
about 40 g/1½ oz fresh flat-
  leaf parsley, thick stems
  removed, leaves chopped

1 tsp cumin seeds, crushed
pepper
warmed pitta breads,
  to serve

to garnish

4 hard-boiled eggs,
  quartered
4 lemon wedges
sumac or crushed red
  pepper flakes

>1 Drain the beans, rinse well and put into a large saucepan. Cover with water and bring to the boil. Boil for 10 minutes, then reduce the heat and simmer for 1½–2 hours, or until very tender. Top up with boiling water if necessary.

>2 Drain the beans and tip into a shallow serving dish. Lightly crush some of them with the back of a wooden spoon.

>3 Add the garlic, lemon juice, olive oil and salt while the beans are still warm. Mix gently, then add the onion, tomatoes and parsley.

>4 Add the cumin seeds and some pepper and gently toss.

>5 Arrange the egg quarters and lemon wedges on top.

>6 Sprinkle with a pinch of sumac.

Serve with fingers of warm pitta bread.

asparagus & egg pastries

serves 4

ingredients

500 g/1 lb 2 oz ready-made
  puff pastry
flour, for dusting
milk, for brushing
300 g/10½ oz slim
  asparagus spears

200 g/7 oz ready-made
  tomato pasta sauce
1 tsp hot smoked paprika
4 eggs
salt and pepper

>1 Roll out the pastry on a lightly floured surface to a 35 x 20-cm/14 x 8-inch rectangle, then cut into four 20 x 9-cm/8 x 3½-inch rectangles.

>2 Line a baking sheet with non-stick baking paper and place the pastry rectangles on the sheet Prick all over with a fork and brush lightly with milk. Chill for 20 minutes.

>3 Snap the woody ends off the asparagus and discard. Bring a saucepan of lightly salted water to the boil. Add the asparagus, bring back to the boil and cook for 2–3 minutes, until almost tender. Drain and refresh in cold water, then drain again. Set aside.

>4 Meanwhile, preheat the oven to 200°C/400°F/Gas Mark 6. Mix the pasta sauce and paprika together and divide between the pastry bases, spreading it out almost to the edges. Bake in the preheated oven for 10–12 minutes until the pastry is puffed around the edges and pale golden in colour.

>5 Remove from the oven and arrange the asparagus on top, leaving space for the egg in the middle of each pastry.

>6 Crack an egg into a cup and slide into the space created. Repeat with the remaining eggs, then return the pastries to the oven for 8 minutes, or until the eggs are just set.

Season the pastries with salt and pepper to taste and serve immediately.

mushrooms & sizzled sage on sourdough toast

serves 4

ingredients

5 tbsp olive oil
2 tbsp roughly chopped
  fresh sage, plus
  16–20 whole small leaves
400 g/14 oz even-sized
  chestnut mushrooms,
  halved
lemon juice
1 large garlic clove,
  thinly sliced
2 tbsp chopped fresh
  flat-leaf parsley
¼ tsp pepper
4 slices sourdough bread
sea salt flakes
vegetarian Parmesan-style
  cheese shavings,
  to garnish

>1 Heat the oil in a large frying pan over a medium–high heat. Add the chopped sage and sizzle for a few seconds. Add the mushrooms and fry for 3–4 minutes, until they are beginning to release their juices.

>2 Add a squeeze of lemon juice, then add the garlic, parsley, pepper and a pinch of salt. Cook for a further 5 minutes.

Sprinkle over some cheese shavings and serve immediately.

> **>3** Meanwhile, toast the bread on both sides. Place on warmed plates and pile the mushrooms on top.

> **>4** Sizzle the whole sage leaves in the oil remaining in the pan over a high heat for a few seconds, until crisp. Scatter over the mushrooms.

95

roasted vegetable & feta cheese wraps

serves 4

ingredients

1 red onion, cut into eighths
1 red pepper, deseeded
  and cut into eighths
1 small aubergine,
  cut into eighths
1 courgette, cut into eighths
4 tbsp extra virgin olive oil
1 garlic clove, crushed
100 g/3½ oz vegetarian feta
  cheese, crumbled
small bunch of fresh mint,
  shredded
4 x 25-cm/10-inch sun-dried
  tomato wraps
salt and pepper

> **>1** Preheat the oven to 220°C/425°F/
> Gas Mark 7. Mix together the vegetables,
> oil, and garlic, season with salt and pepper
> and arrange in a single layer on a non-stick
> baking tray. Roast in the preheated oven
> for 15–20 minutes, or until golden and
> cooked through.

> **>2** Remove from the oven and leave to
> cool, then add the cheese and mint
> and mix to combine.

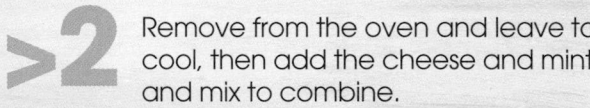

Roll up the wraps, cut them in half and serve immediately.

>3 Preheat a non-stick frying pan or griddle pan until almost smoking, then add the wraps one at a time and cook for 10 seconds on each side.

>4 Divide the vegetable and cheese mixture between the wraps, placing it along the middle of each wrap.

leafy greens, leek & asparagus stir-fry

serves 4–6

ingredients

500 g/1 lb 2 oz mixed leafy greens, such as pak choi, cavolo nero, chard and spinach
225 g/8 oz asparagus
5 tbsp groundnut oil

3-cm/1¼-inch piece fresh ginger, diced
½–1 fresh green or red chilli, deseeded and diced
3 large garlic cloves, peeled and thinly sliced

6 baby leeks, lower green part included, sliced into rounds
3–4 tbsp vegetable stock or water
2 tbsp soy sauce
½ tsp salt

small handful fresh coriander leaves
1 tsp sesame seeds
1 tbsp toasted sesame oil pepper
boiled rice or noodles, to serve

> **1** Cut away the stalks and large central ribs from the greens. Slice the stalks into 1-cm/½-inch pieces. Stack the leaves and slice into ribbons.

> **2** Snap off the woody ends from the asparagus and discard. Chop the stems into 2-cm/¾-inch pieces. Leave the tips whole.

> **3** Heat a large wok over a high heat and add the groundnut oil. When almost smoking, add the ginger, chilli and garlic. Stir-fry for 30 seconds.

> **4** Add the leeks, asparagus and the chopped stalks from the greens. Add stock to moisten and stir-fry for a further 2 minutes.

>5 Add the sliced leaves, soy sauce, salt and
a little pepper and stir-fry for 3 minutes.

>6 Stir in the coriander, sesame seeds and
sesame oil and stir-fry for 30 seconds.

Serve immediately with boiled rice.

wild mushroom omelette

serves 2

ingredients

1 tsp extra virgin olive oil
1 small onion, cut into
  wedges
2–3 garlic cloves, crushed
85 g/3 oz mixed wild
  mushrooms, halved if large
85 g/3 oz closed-cup
  mushrooms, sliced
1 courgette, grated
2 eggs
2 egg whites
2 tbsp water
1 yellow pepper, deseeded
  and cut into strips
1 tbsp grated vegetarian
  Parmesan-style cheese
  (optional)
salt and pepper
1 tbsp shredded fresh basil
rocket, to garnish
wholemeal bread, to serve

>1 Heat the oil in a large non-stick frying pan. Add the onion and garlic, cover and cook, stirring occasionally, for 3 minutes. Add the mushrooms and cook for a further 4–5 minutes, or until the mushrooms have softened slightly. Add the courgette.

>2 Beat together the eggs, egg whites and water with salt and pepper to taste.

Cut the omelette into wedges, garnish with rocket and serve with wholemeal bread.

>3 Pour the egg mixture into the frying pan. Increase the heat slightly and cook, using a fork or spatula to draw the egg into the centre of the pan from the edges.

>4 When the omelette is set on the base, sprinkle over the yellow pepper, the cheese, if using, and the basil. Cook for a further 3–4 minutes, or until set to your liking.

warm butternut squash, mushroom & spinach salad

serves 4

ingredients

1 small butternut squash
5 tbsp olive oil
squeeze of lemon juice
2–3 Portobello mushrooms,
   thinly sliced

½ tsp coriander seeds,
   crushed
40 g/1½ oz unskinned
   almonds, halved
   lengthways

½ tbsp balsamic vinegar
juice of 1 small orange
4 handfuls baby spinach
2 tbsp snipped chives
sea salt flakes and pepper

> **1** Slice the squash where the neck meets the bulbous end. Slice the neck lengthways into quarters. Slice the end lengthways in half. Remove the peel and seeds.

> **2** Slice the neck pieces lengthways into thin segments. Slice the end pieces crossways into thin semi-circles.

> **3** Heat the oil in a large frying pan over a medium–high heat. Add the squash in a single layer and fry, turning, for 5–7 minutes, until lightly browned. You will need to do this in batches.

> **4** Sprinkle with salt and pepper and lemon juice. Using a slotted spoon, transfer to a large sieve set over a bowl and leave to drain.

>**5** Add the mushrooms and coriander seeds to the pan and fry for 5 minutes. Season with salt and pepper and sprinkle with a little lemon juice. Add to the squash in the sieve.

>**6** Add the almonds to the oil remaining in the pan and cook, stirring, until brown. Remove from the pan and set aside.

>**7** Pour the drained juices from the vegetables into the pan. Stir in the vinegar, orange juice and a splash of water. Stir for a few seconds.

>**8** Arrange the spinach on serving plates and pile the squash and mushrooms on top.

Scatter over the almonds and chives, pour
over the pan juices and serve while still warm.

spring onion, pea & ricotta tarts

makes 12

ingredients

pastry

200 g/7 oz plain flour,
  plus extra for dusting
pinch of salt
125 g/4½ oz butter, diced,
  plus extra for greasing
1 egg yolk

filling

100 g/3½ oz vegetarian
  pecorino cheese
250 g/9 oz vegetarian
  ricotta cheese
1 egg, beaten
12 spring onions,
  finely chopped

2 tbsp fresh shelled peas,
  lightly cooked and cooled
1 tsp green peppercorns
  in brine, drained and very
  finely chopped
salt and pepper

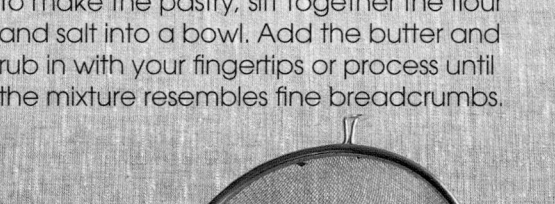

>1 To make the pastry, sift together the flour and salt into a bowl. Add the butter and rub in with your fingertips or process until the mixture resembles fine breadcrumbs.

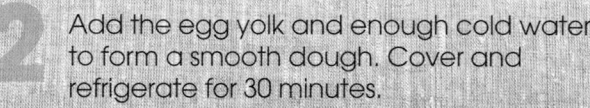

>2 Add the egg yolk and enough cold water to form a smooth dough. Cover and refrigerate for 30 minutes.

>3 Meanwhile, preheat the oven to 190°C/375°F/Gas Mark 5. Lightly grease a deep, 12 cup muffin tin.

>4 Roll out the pastry on a lightly floured work surface to a thickness of 3–4 mm/¼ inch. Using a round pastry cutter, cut out rounds large enough to line the cups of the tin.

>5 Gently press the pastry cases into the cups. Line each pastry case with a small piece of baking paper and fill with baking beans. Bake in the preheated oven for 4–5 minutes, until golden and crisp. Remove the paper and beans.

>6 Meanwhile, to make the filling, grate the pecorino cheese finely. Mix together the ricotta cheese and pecorino cheese in a large bowl.

>7 Add the egg, spring onions, peas and peppercorns. Season to taste with salt and pepper.

>8 Spoon the filling into the pastry cases and bake for 10 minutes, or until golden. Leave to stand in the tin for a few minutes.

Remove the tarts from the tin and serve warm.

eggs with fried tomato, onion & peppers

serves 4

ingredients

4 large ripe tomatoes

1½ tbsp rapeseed oil

1 large onion, finely
chopped

½ tsp coriander seeds,
crushed

½ tsp caraway seeds,
crushed

2 red peppers, deseeded
and diced

¼ tsp dried chilli flakes

1 large garlic clove,
thinly sliced

4 eggs

sea salt and pepper

chopped fresh flat-leaf
parsley, to garnish

>**1** Put the tomatoes into a shallow bowl and cover with boiling water. Leave for 30 seconds, then drain.

>**2** Slip off the tomato skins and discard. Chop the flesh, reserving the seeds and juice.

>**3** Heat the oil in a large, non-stick frying pan over a medium heat. Add the onion, coriander seeds and caraway seeds. Fry, stirring occasionally, for about 10 minutes, until the onion is soft and golden.

>**4** Stir in the red peppers and chilli flakes. Fry for about 5 minutes, until soft.

113

>5 Add the garlic and tomatoes with their seeds and juices and season with salt and pepper. Simmer, uncovered, over a low heat for 10 minutes.

>6 Crack the eggs over the surface. Cover and cook for a further 3–4 minutes, or until the eggs are set.

Season with salt and pepper to taste, sprinkle
with parsley and serve immediately.

couscous with roast cherry tomatoes & pine nuts

serves 4

ingredients
300 g/10½ oz cherry
 tomatoes
3 tbsp olive oil
125 g/4½ oz couscous
200 ml/7 fl oz boiling water
30 g/1 oz pine nuts, toasted
5 tbsp roughly chopped
 fresh mint
finely grated rind of 1 lemon
½ tbsp lemon juice
salt and pepper
crisp green salad and
 vegetarian feta cheese,
 to serve

>1 Preheat the oven to 220°C/425°F/
Gas Mark 7. Place the tomatoes and
1 tablespoon of the oil in a ovenproof dish.
Toss together, then roast for 7–8 minutes in
the preheated oven until the tomatoes
are soft and the skins have burst. Leave to
stand for 5 minutes.

>2 Put the couscous in a heatproof bowl.
Pour over the boiling water, cover and
leave to stand for 8–10 minutes, until soft
and the liquid has been absorbed.

Serve the couscous warm or cold, with a green salad and some feta cheese.

>3 Fluff up the couscous with a fork.

>4 Add the tomatoes and their juices, the pine nuts, mint, lemon rind, lemon juice and the remaining oil. Season with salt and pepper, then gently toss together.

117

midweek & family suppers

caramelized sweet potatoes

serves 4

ingredients

450 g/1 lb sweet potatoes,
  washed but not peeled
55 g/2 oz butter, plus extra
  for greasing
55 g/2 oz brown sugar,
  maple syrup or honey
2 tbsp orange or pineapple
  juice
55 g/2 oz pineapple pieces
  (optional)
pinch of ground cinnamon,
  nutmeg or mixed spice
  (optional)
salt

> **>1** Bring a large saucepan of lightly salted water to the boil. Add the sweet potatoes, bring back to the boil and cook for about 30–45 minutes, until just tender. Remove from the heat and drain well. Leave to cool slightly, then peel.

> **>2** Preheat the oven to 200°C/400°F/ Gas Mark 6. Grease an ovenproof dish. Thickly slice the sweet potatoes and arrange in a single overlapping layer in the prepared dish.

Remove from the oven and serve hot, straight from the dish.

>3 Cut the butter into small cubes and dot over the top.

>4 Sprinkle with the sugar and orange juice. Add the pineapple pieces, and spices, if using. Bake in the preheated oven for 30–40 minutes, basting occasionally, until golden brown.

new potato, rosemary & rocket pizza

serves 4

ingredients

280 g/10 oz small waxy
  potatoes, unpeeled
2 tbsp olive oil, plus extra
  for greasing
2 garlic cloves, thinly sliced
1½ tbsp chopped fresh
  rosemary leaves
1 ready-made 30-cm/
  12-inch pizza base
85 g/3 oz vegetarian
  smoked cheese, coarsely
  grated
115 g/4 oz vegetarian
  Gruyère cheese, coarsely
  grated
8 Kalamata olives, stoned
  and halved
handful of rocket
sea salt and pepper

>1 Preheat the oven to 240°C/475°F/
Gas Mark 9. Bring a saucepan of lightly
salted water to the boil. Add the potatoes,
bring back to the boil and blanch for
3 minutes. Drain, then thinly slice.

>2 Heat the oil in a large frying pan over
a medium–high heat. Add the potatoes
and fry for 3–4 minutes, until lightly
browned. Add the garlic, 1 tablespoon
of the rosemary, and salt and pepper to
taste. Fry for a further 1 minute.

Scatter over the rocket and serve immediately.

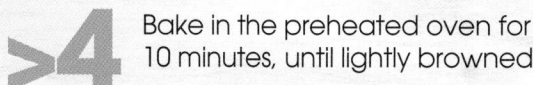

>**3** Place the pizza base on a baking sheet. Sprinkle with two thirds of the smoked cheese and the Gruyère cheese. Arrange the potatoes on top. Add the remaining cheese, the olives and the remaining rosemary.

>**4** Bake in the preheated oven for 10 minutes, until lightly browned.

pumpkin & chestnut risotto

serves 4

ingredients

1 tbsp olive oil
40 g/1½ oz butter
1 small onion,
  finely chopped

225 g/8 oz pumpkin, diced
225 g/8 oz chestnuts,
  cooked and shelled
280 g/10 oz risotto rice
150 ml/5 fl oz dry white wine

1 tsp crumbled saffron
  threads (optional),
  dissolved in 4 tbsp
  of the stock
1 litre/1¾ pints simmering
  vegetable stock

85 g/3 oz vegetarian
  Parmesan-style cheese,
  freshly grated, plus extra
  for serving
salt and pepper

> **1** Heat the oil with 25 g/1 oz of the butter in a deep saucepan over a medium heat until the butter has melted. Stir in the onion and pumpkin and cook, stirring occasionally, for 5 minutes, or until the onion is soft and starting to turn golden and the pumpkin begins to colour.

> **2** Roughly chop the chestnuts and add to the mixture. Stir thoroughly to coat.

> **3** Reduce the heat, add the rice and mix to coat in oil and butter. Cook, stirring constantly, for 2–3 minutes, or until the grains are translucent. Add the wine and cook, stirring constantly, for 1 minute, until it has reduced.

> **4** Add the saffron liquid to the rice, if using, and cook, stirring constantly, until the liquid has been absorbed.

>5 Gradually add the simmering stock, a ladleful at a time, stirring constantly. Add more liquid as the rice absorbs each addition. Increase the heat to medium so that the liquid bubbles.

Cook for 20 minutes, or until all the liquid has been absorbed and the rice is creamy. Season to taste with salt and pepper.

>6 Remove the risotto from the heat and add the remaining butter. Mix well, then stir in the cheese until it melts. Adjust the seasoning, if necessary.

Spoon the risotto onto four warmed
plates and serve immediately, sprinkled
with grated cheese.

spiced parsnip gratin with ginger cream

serves 4

ingredients

butter, for greasing
3 large parsnips, about
750 g/1 lb 10 oz,
thinly sliced
425 ml/15 fl oz double
cream
250 ml/9 fl oz vegetable
stock
1 garlic clove, crushed
2.5-cm/1-inch piece fresh
ginger, roughly chopped
and crushed in a garlic
press
¼ tsp freshly ground white
pepper
⅛ tsp freshly grated nutmeg,
plus extra to garnish
sea salt
snipped chives, to garnish

> **1** Lightly grease a large gratin dish. Place the parsnips in a steamer basket set over a saucepan of boiling water. Steam for 3 minutes, until barely tender, shaking halfway through cooking. Tip into the prepared dish and lightly season with salt.

> **2** Preheat the oven to 180°C/350°F/Gas Mark 4. Gently heat the cream and stock in a saucepan with the garlic and ginger. Do not allow the mixture to boil. Add the pepper, nutmeg and sea salt to taste.

Sprinkle with a little more nutmeg and some chives and serve.

> **>3** Pour the hot cream mixture over the parsnips. Cover the dish with foil and bake in the preheated oven for 20 minutes, with an oven tray underneath to catch any drips.

> **>4** Remove the foil and bake for a further 15–20 minutes, until golden on top.

spaghetti with fresh pea pesto & broad beans

serves 4

ingredients

250 g/9 oz shelled broad
  beans
500 g/1 lb 2 oz dried
  spaghetti
salt and pepper

pea pesto

300 g/10½ oz fresh shelled
  peas
75 ml/2½ fl oz extra virgin
  olive oil
2 garlic cloves, crushed
100 g/3½ oz freshly grated
  vegetarian Parmesan-
  style cheese, plus extra
  shavings, to serve
100 g/3½ oz blanched
  almonds, chopped
pinch of sugar
salt and pepper

> **>1** To make the pesto, bring a saucepan of water to the boil. Add the peas, bring back to the boil and cook for 2–3 minutes, until just tender. Drain and transfer to a blender or food processor.

> **>2** Add the oil, garlic and cheese and process to a coarse paste. Add the almonds and process again. Add the sugar and season to taste with salt and pepper. Set aside.

Turn out into a serving bowl, add a coarse grinding of pepper and serve immediately with cheese shavings scattered over the top.

>3 Bring a saucepan of lightly salted water to the boil. Add the beans, bring back to the boil and cook until just tender. Drain and leave to cool. Peel off the dull skins.

>4 Bring a separate saucepan of lightly salted water to the boil. Add the spaghetti, bring back to the boil and cook according to the packet instructions, until tender but still firm to the bite. Drain, stir in the broad beans and toss with the pesto.

131

bean & tomato casserole with parmesan toasts

serves 4

ingredients

350 g/12 oz borlotti beans, soaked overnight

4 tbsp extra virgin olive oil, plus extra for drizzling

25 g/1 oz butter

1 large onion, thinly sliced

15–20 fresh sage leaves, sliced

2 large garlic cloves, thinly sliced

1 tbsp tomato purée

800 g/1 lb 12 oz canned chopped tomatoes

300 ml/10 fl oz vegetable stock

4 tbsp chopped fresh flat-leaf parsley

50 g/1¾ oz coarsely grated vegetarian Parmesan-style cheese

8 thin slices ciabatta, toasted

sea salt and pepper

small fresh sage sprigs, to garnish

>1 Drain the beans, rinse well and put them into a large saucepan. Cover with water and bring to the boil. Boil for 10 minutes, then reduce the heat and simmer for 45–60 minutes, or until tender. Drain.

>2 Heat the oil and butter in a large saucepan over a medium heat. Add the onion and sage and fry for 5 minutes, until the onion is translucent. Add the garlic and fry for 2 minutes, until just coloured.

>3 Add the tomato purée and fry for 1 minute, stirring.

>4 Stir in the tomatoes, beans and stock and season with salt and pepper. Bring to the boil, then reduce the heat and simmer, partially covered, for 20 minutes.

>5 Add the parsley and half the cheese.

>6 Ladle the beans into shallow soup plates. Top each plate with 2 slices of toasted ciabatta. Drizzle the bread with the remaining oil and sprinkle with cheese.

Garnish with sage sprigs and serve immediately.

falafel burgers

serves 4

ingredients

800 g/1 lb 12 oz canned
   chickpeas, drained and
   rinsed
1 small onion, chopped
juice and grated rind of
   1 lime
2 tsp ground coriander
2 tsp ground cumin
6 tbsp plain flour
4 tbsp olive oil
watercress, to garnish
ready-made tomato salsa,
   to serve

> **>1** Put the chickpeas, onion, lime juice and rind and the spices into a food processor and process to a coarse paste.

> **>2** Tip out onto a clean work surface and shape into 4 patties.

Garnish with watercress and serve immediately with tomato salsa.

>3 Spread out the flour on a large flat plate and turn the patties in it to coat.

>4 Heat the oil in a large frying pan, add the patties and cook for 2 minutes on each side, until crisp.

rigatoni with courgette, tomato & mascarpone

serves 4

ingredients

4 courgettes, roughly
 chopped
2½ tbsp olive oil
1 onion, finely chopped

1 garlic clove, crushed
800 g/1 lb 12 oz canned
 chopped tomatoes
6 sun-dried tomatoes,
 chopped

225 ml/8 fl oz vegetable
 stock
½ tsp dried oregano
280 g/10 oz dried rigatoni
 pasta

125 g/4½ oz mascarpone
 cheese
large handful of fresh basil
 leaves, torn into pieces
salt and pepper

>1 Preheat the oven to 200°C/400°F/ Gas Mark 6. Place the courgettes and 1½ tablespoons of the oil in a large ovenproof dish.

>2 Toss together and spread out in a single layer. Roast in the preheated oven for 15–20 minutes, until tender and lightly browned.

>3 Meanwhile, heat the remaining oil in a saucepan. Add the onion and garlic and cook very gently for 5 minutes until soft. Add the canned tomatoes, sun-dried tomatoes, stock and oregano. Simmer for 10 minutes until the liquid has reduced slightly.

>4 Bring a large saucepan of lightly salted water to the boil. Add the pasta, bring back to the boil and cook according to the packet instructions, until tender but still firm to the bite. Drain well, then return to the pan.

 **5** Add the mascarpone cheese to the hot tomato sauce and stir until melted and smooth. Season well with salt and pepper.

6 Add the sauce to the pasta with the courgettes and basil.

Toss well until all the ingredients are coated
with sauce and serve immediately.

quinoa with roasted vegetables

serves 2

ingredients

- 2 peppers (any colour), deseeded and cut into chunky pieces
- 1 large courgette, cut into chunks
- 1 small fennel bulb, cut into slim wedges
- 1 tbsp olive oil
- 2 tsp very finely chopped fresh rosemary
- 1 tsp chopped fresh thyme
- 100 g/3½ oz quinoa
- 350 ml/12 fl oz vegetable stock
- 2 garlic cloves, crushed
- 3 tbsp chopped fresh flat-leaf parsley
- 40 g/1½ oz pine nuts, toasted
- salt and pepper

>1 Preheat the oven to 200°C/400°F/ Gas Mark 6. Arrange the vegetables in a single layer in a large roasting tin.

>2 Drizzle the oil over the vegetables and scatter over the rosemary and thyme. Season well with salt and pepper and mix well with clean hands.

Toss well together and serve.

Roast in the preheated oven for 25–30 minutes, until tender and lightly charred. Meanwhile, place the quinoa, stock and garlic in a saucepan. Bring to the boil, cover and reduce the heat. Simmer for 12–15 minutes, until the quinoa is tender and most of the stock has been absorbed.

Remove the vegetables from the oven. Tip the quinoa into the roasting tin. Add the parsley and pine nuts.

asparagus & pea frittata

serves 3–4

ingredients

8 asparagus spears
350 g/12 oz peas, shelled
8 eggs
½ tsp sea salt
1 tbsp olive oil

large knob of butter
8 spring onions, trimmed
 and finely sliced
pepper
green salad, to serve

> **1** Snap the woody ends from the asparagus and discard. Chop the stems into 1-cm/½-inch pieces and chop the tips into 2.5-cm/1-inch pieces.

> **2** Put the asparagus and peas into a steamer basket set over a saucepan of boiling water. Steam for 3 minutes. Remove from the heat and reserve.

> **3** Beat the eggs well. Add the salt and some pepper.

> **4** Heat the oil and butter in a 24-cm/9½-inch non-stick frying pan over a medium heat. Add the spring onions and fry for 2 minutes. Stir in the peas and asparagus. Pour in the eggs, stirring to distribute the vegetables evenly.

>5 Cover the pan and cook over a medium–low heat for 10–12 minutes, or until the eggs are almost set. Place under a hot grill and cook for a further 3–5 minutes, or until the top is set.

>6 Turn out onto a serving plate and cut into wedges.

Serve hot or warm with a green salad.

roasted squash & celeriac with balsamic glaze

serves 2–3

ingredients

1 kg/2 lb 4 oz dense-fleshed
squash, such as Kabocha
or Crown Prince
½ celeriac, peeled
5 tbsp rapeseed oil
1 tbsp thick balsamic
vinegar
1 tsp coriander seeds,
crushed
1 tsp fresh thyme leaves
25 g/1 oz butter
sea salt flakes and pepper
steamed broccoli or green
cabbage, to serve

>1 Preheat the oven to 200°C/400°F/
Gas Mark 6. Slice the squash into quarters.
Cut away the peel and scoop out the
seeds. Cut each quarter crossways into
2 pieces. Cut the celeriac into quarters
and then into chunks smaller than the
squash pieces.

>2 Whisk together the oil, vinegar, coriander
seeds and thyme with some pepper and
a good pinch of salt in a large bowl. Add
the squash and celeriac, turning in the
mixture until well coated.

Serve immediately with steamed broccoli.

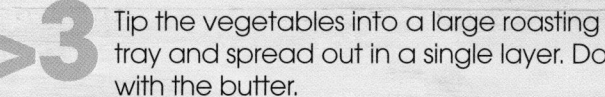

>3 Tip the vegetables into a large roasting tray and spread out in a single layer. Dot with the butter.

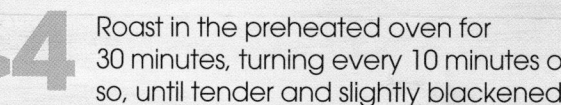

>4 Roast in the preheated oven for 30 minutes, turning every 10 minutes or so, until tender and slightly blackened.

potato gnocchi with walnut pesto

serves 4

ingredients

450 g/1 lb floury potatoes, washed but not peeled
55 g/2 oz freshly grated vegetarian Parmesan-style cheese

1 egg, beaten
200 g/7 oz plain flour, plus extra for dusting
salt and pepper

walnut pesto

40 g/1½ oz fresh flat-leaf parsley, chopped
2 tbsp capers, rinsed and chopped
2 garlic cloves, chopped
175 ml/6 fl oz extra virgin olive oil

70 g/2½ oz walnut pieces
40 g/1½ oz freshly grated vegetarian Parmesan-style cheese
salt and pepper

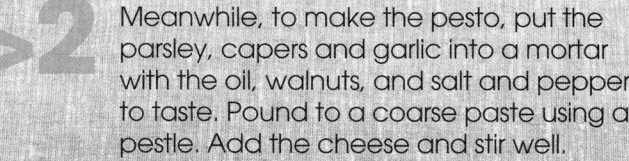

> 1 Bring a large saucepan of lightly salted water to the boil. Add the potatoes, bring back to the boil and cook for 30–35 minutes, until tender. Drain well and leave to cool slightly.

> 2 Meanwhile, to make the pesto, put the parsley, capers and garlic into a mortar with the oil, walnuts, and salt and pepper to taste. Pound to a coarse paste using a pestle. Add the cheese and stir well.

> 3 When the potatoes are cool enough to handle, peel off the skins and pass the flesh through a sieve into a large bowl or press through a potato ricer. While still hot, season well with salt and pepper and add the cheese.

> 4 Beat in the egg and sift in the flour. Lightly mix together, then turn out onto a lightly floured work surface. Lightly knead until the mixture becomes a smooth dough. If it is too sticky, add a little more flour.

151

> **5** Using your hands, roll out the dough on a lightly floured work surface into a long log.

> **6** Cut into 2.5-cm/1-inch pieces and gently press with a fork to give the traditional ridged effect. Transfer to a floured baking sheet and cover with a clean tea towel while you make the remaining gnocchi.

> **7** Bring a large saucepan of water to the boil, add the gnocchi, in small batches, and cook for 1–2 minutes.

> **8** Remove with a slotted spoon and transfer to a warmed dish to keep warm while you cook the remaining gnocchi.

Serve the gnocchi on warmed plates,
topped with a good spoonful of the pesto.

polenta with tomatoes & garlic sauce

serves 4

ingredients

700 ml/1¼ pints vegetable
  stock or water
175 g/6 oz quick-cook
  polenta
25 g/1 oz butter
3 tbsp snipped fresh chives

2 tbsp chopped fresh
  flat-leaf parsley
olive oil, for brushing
4 plum tomatoes, sliced
salt and pepper

garlic sauce

2 thick slices of French
  bread, crusts removed
3 garlic cloves, chopped
½ tsp salt
115 g/4 oz walnut pieces

3 tbsp lemon juice
7 tbsp olive oil

> 1 Pour the stock into a large saucepan, bring to the boil and add 1 teaspoon of salt. Add the polenta and cook over a medium heat, stirring constantly, for 5 minutes, until it starts to come away from the sides of the pan.

> 2 Remove the pan from the heat and beat in the butter, chives and parsley and season to taste with pepper. Pour the polenta into a greased dish and spread out evenly. Leave to cool and set.

> 3 To make the sauce, tear the bread into pieces and place in a bowl. Cover with cold water and soak for 10 minutes.

> 4 Put the garlic cloves into a mortar with the salt and pound with a pestle to make a paste. Work in the walnuts.

>5 Squeeze out the bread, work it into the paste, then work in the lemon juice. Stir in the oil until the sauce is thick and creamy. Transfer to a bowl, cover with clingfilm and set aside.

>6 Brush the grill with oil and preheat. Cut the set polenta into wedges or rounds. Season the tomatoes with salt and pepper. When the grill is hot add the polenta and tomatoes, and cook for 4–5 minutes.

Divide the polenta and tomatoes between warmed plates, spoon over the sauce and serve immediately.

roasted cauliflower, tomato & olive gratin

serves 4

ingredients

4 tbsp olive oil
50 g/1¾ oz butter, plus extra
  for greasing
1 large onion, chopped
1½ tsp fresh thyme leaves
3 garlic cloves, thinly sliced

800 g/1 lb 12 oz canned
  chopped tomatoes
2–3 slivers lemon peel
100 g/3½ oz coarse
  ciabatta breadcrumbs

10–12 Kalamata olives,
  pitted and chopped
4 tbsp chopped fresh
  flat-leaf parsley
1 large cauliflower

25 g/1 oz coarsely grated
  vegetarian Parmesan-
  style cheese
sea salt and pepper

> **1** Heat 2 tablespoons of the oil and half the butter in a high-sided frying pan over a medium heat. Add the onion and thyme and fry for 5 minutes, until the onion is translucent. Add the garlic and fry for 1–2 minutes, until just coloured.

> **2** Stir in the tomatoes and lemon peel. Season with salt and pepper, then simmer, stirring, for 20 minutes, until thickened.

> **3** Preheat the oven to 200°C/400°F/Gas Mark 6. Grease an ovenproof dish with butter. Combine the breadcrumbs, olives and parsley in a bowl. Mix in the remaining oil.

> **4** Cut the cauliflower into quarters. Cut out the core. Break the florets into clumps and pack in a single layer in the prepared dish. Season with salt and pepper.

>5 Pour in the tomato sauce, pushing it into the spaces between the florets. Sprinkle the breadcrumb mixture evenly over the top. Dot with the remaining butter.

>6 Cover with foil and roast in the preheated oven for 35 minutes. Remove the foil and roast for a further 15 minutes, until the cauliflower is tender-crisp and the crumbs are golden.

Sprinkle with cheese and serve immediately.

carrot tarte tatin

serves 4

ingredients
600 g/1 lb 5 oz young
  carrots, cut into
  2.5-cm/1-inch chunks
2 tbsp clear honey
25 g/1 oz butter
1 small bunch fresh thyme,
  chopped
350 g/12 oz ready-made
  puff pastry, thawed if
  frozen
plain flour, for dusting
salt and pepper

> **>1** Bring a large saucepan of lightly salted water to the boil. Add the carrots, bring back to the boil and cook for 10–15 minutes, until just tender. Drain, toss with the honey, butter and thyme and season to taste with salt and pepper.

> **>2** Preheat the oven to 200°C/400°F/ Gas Mark 6. Spoon the carrots over the base of a 20-cm/8-inch tarte tatin tin or round cake tin with a depth of about 3 cm/1¼ inches. Roast in the preheated oven for 15 minutes, or until the carrots are caramelized.

Cut the tart into slices and serve immediately.

>3 Roll out the pastry on a floured work surface into a round large enough to fit the tin and give a 2-cm/¾-inch overlap. Lay the pastry carefully over the carrots and tuck the edges down between the carrots and the side of the tin to make a border. Bake in the oven for 15 minutes, or until the pastry is puffed and golden.

>4 Remove the tart from the oven and turn the tin over onto a plate to release.

special occasions

mushrooms with pasta, pine nuts & parmesan

serves 4

ingredients

2 tbsp olive oil
25 g/1 oz butter
2 shallots, chopped
2 large garlic cloves,
   thinly sliced

450 g/1 lb chestnut or
Portobello mushrooms,
thickly sliced, halved if
large
1 tsp chopped marjoram
grated rind of ½ lemon

450 g/1 lb dried
pappardelle or other wide
ribbon pasta
75 g/2¾ oz pine nuts,
toasted
300 ml/10 fl oz whipping
cream

6 tbsp freshly grated
vegetarian Parmesan-
style cheese, plus extra
to serve
2 tbsp chopped fresh
flat-leaf parsley
sea salt and pepper

>1 Heat the oil and butter together in a large frying pan. Add the shallots and fry over a medium heat for about 2 minutes, until soft. Add the garlic and fry for a further 1–2 minutes, until lightly coloured.

>2 Add the mushrooms and marjoram to the pan. Increase the heat to medium–high. Fry for 5–7 minutes, stirring, until the mushrooms start to release their liquid.

>3 Sprinkle with the lemon rind. Season with salt and plenty of pepper. Cook for a further 1–2 minutes, or until the liquid has evaporated.

>4 Meanwhile, bring a large saucepan of lightly salted water to the boil and cook the pasta according to the packet instructions.

>5 Add the pine nuts, cream and cheese to the mushrooms in the pan. Stir until heated through. Check the seasoning.

>6 Drain the pasta and tip into a large warmed serving dish. Pour the mushroom mixture over the top and sprinkle with the parsley.

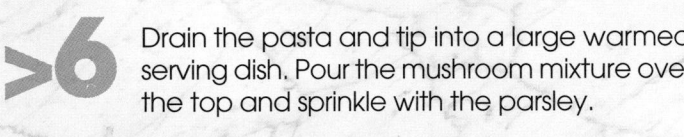

Serve immediately with extra cheese for
handing round.

asparagus & sun-dried tomato risotto

serves 4

ingredients

1 tbsp olive oil
40 g/1½ oz butter
1 small onion, finely
  chopped
6 sun-dried tomatoes,
  thinly sliced

280 g/10 oz risotto rice
150 ml/5 fl oz dry white wine
1 litre/1¾ pints simmering
  vegetable stock
225 g/8 oz fresh asparagus
  spears, cooked

85 g/3 oz freshly grated
  vegetarian Parmesan-style
  cheese, plus extra
  to garnish
salt and pepper
lemon rind, to garnish

> 1
Heat the oil with 25 g/1 oz of the butter in a deep saucepan over a medium heat until the butter has melted.

> 2
Stir in the onion and sun-dried tomatoes and cook, stirring occasionally, for 5 minutes, until the onion is soft and starting to turn golden. Do not brown.

> 3
Reduce the heat, add the rice and mix to coat in oil and butter. Cook, stirring constantly, for 2–3 minutes, or until the grains are translucent.

> 4
Add the wine and cook, stirring constantly, until it has reduced.

>5 Gradually add the hot stock, a ladleful at a time. Stir constantly, adding more liquid as the rice absorbs each addition. Increase the heat to medium so that the liquid bubbles. Cook for 20 minutes, or until all the liquid is absorbed and the rice is creamy. Season to taste.

>6 Meanwhile, cut most of the asparagus into pieces about 2.5 cm/1 inch long, reserving several whole spears to garnish. Carefully fold the cut pieces of asparagus into the risotto for the last 5 minutes of cooking time.

>7 Remove the risotto from the heat and add the remaining butter. Mix well, then stir in the cheese until it melts.

>8 Spoon the risotto into individual warmed serving dishes and garnish with the reserved asparagus spears.

Sprinkle some cheese and lemon rind over the risotto and serve immediately.

jerusalem artichoke & hazelnut gratin

serves 4

ingredients

750 g/1 lb 10 oz Jerusalem
  artichokes
squeeze of lemon juice
25 g/1 oz butter, plus extra
  for greasing
4 tbsp skinned hazelnuts,
  roughly chopped

40 g/1½ oz coarse ciabatta
  breadcrumbs
sea salt and pepper
steamed French beans, to
  serve

garlic cream

250 ml/9 fl oz whipping
  cream
7 large garlic cloves, peeled
  and lightly crushed
sliver of lemon peel
squeeze of lemon juice

> **1** To make the garlic cream, heat the cream, garlic and lemon peel in a saucepan over a medium heat, then simmer for about 5 minutes, until slightly reduced. Remove from the heat and leave to stand in a warm place.

> **2** Peel the artichokes, dropping them into water with a squeeze of lemon juice. Cut in half if they are large. Place in a steamer basket set over a saucepan of boiling water and steam for 8–10 minutes, until just tender at the edges. Leave to cool, then slice fairly thickly.

> **3** Strain the garlic cream into a jug, Add the lemon juice and season to taste.

> **4** Preheat the oven to 190°C/375°F/ Gas Mark 5. Grease a 2-litre/3½-pint baking dish with butter. Arrange half the artichoke slices in the base of the prepared dish. Season with salt and pepper. Sprinkle with the nuts, then top with the remaining artichokes and a little more seasoning.

>5 Pour over the warm garlic cream. Sprinkle with the breadcrumbs and dot with the butter.

>6 Bake in the preheated oven for 30–35 minutes, until the artichokes are tender and the topping is golden and bubbling.

Serve hot with steamed French beans.

caramelized onion tart

serves 4–6

ingredients
100 g/3½ oz unsalted butter
600 g/1 lb 5 oz onions,
    thinly sliced
2 eggs
100 ml/3½ fl oz double
    cream
100 g/3½ oz vegetarian
    Gruyère cheese, grated
20-cm/8-inch ready-baked
    pastry case
100 g/3½ oz coarsely grated
    vegetarian Parmesan-style
    cheese
salt and pepper

> **1** Melt the butter in a heavy-based frying pan over a medium heat. Add the onions and cook, stirring frequently to avoid burning, for 30 minutes, or until well-browned and caramelized. Remove the onions from the pan and set aside.

> **2** Preheat the oven to 190°C/375°F/ Gas Mark 5. Beat the eggs in a large bowl. Stir in the cream and season to taste with salt and pepper. Add the Gruyère cheese and mix well. Stir in the cooked onions.

Cut the tart into slices and serve hot or at room temperature.

>**3** Pour the egg and onion mixture into the baked pastry case and sprinkle with the Parmesan-style cheese.

>**4** Place on a baking sheet and bake in the preheated oven for 15–20 minutes, until the filling has set and is beginning to brown. Remove from the oven and leave to rest for at least 10 minutes.

chickpea, aubergine & red pepper casserole

serves 6

ingredients

1 tsp cumin seeds
2 tsp coriander seeds
2 tsp dried oregano
25 g/1 oz shelled Brazil nuts,
  roughly chopped

1 red pepper, halved and
  deseeded
1 aubergine, thickly sliced
3 tbsp olive oil, plus extra for
  brushing

2 onions, chopped
2 garlic cloves, chopped
400 g/14 oz canned
  chopped tomatoes
400 g/14 oz cooked
  chickpeas

450 ml/16 fl oz vegetable
  stock
sea salt and pepper
3 tbsp chopped fresh
  flat-leaf parsley, to garnish

> **1** Put the cumin seeds and coriander seeds into a dry frying pan over a medium heat and fry until fragrant. Add the oregano, fry for a few seconds, then immediately remove the mixture from the pan.

> **2** Put the seed mixture and the Brazil nuts into a blender and grind to a powder. Set aside. Preheat the grill to high.

> **3** Put the red pepper cut-side down on a roasting tray with the aubergine slices. Brush the aubergine slices with oil. Place under the preheated grill for 7–10 minutes, turning the aubergine slices once, until the aubergine is golden on both sides and the red pepper is blackened.

> **4** Cover the red pepper with a clean tea towel for 10 minutes to loosen the skin. Peel off the skin.

> **5** Slice the grilled vegetables into bite-sized chunks.

> **6** Heat the oil in a heavy-based casserole over a medium heat. Add the onions and fry for 5 minutes, until translucent.

> **7** Stir in the powdered seed mixture and garlic and fry for a further 2–3 minutes.

> **8** Add the tomatoes, chickpeas, red pepper, aubergines and stock and season with salt and pepper. Cover, bring to the boil, then reduce the heat and simmer for 45 minutes.

Sprinkle with the parsley and serve hot.

leek & goat's cheese crêpes

makes 8

ingredients

25 g/1 oz unsalted butter

½ tbsp sunflower oil

200 g/7 oz leeks, halved lengthways, rinsed and finely shredded

freshly grated nutmeg, to taste

1 tbsp finely snipped fresh chives

8 ready-made savoury crêpes

85 g/3 oz vegetarian soft goat's cheese, rind removed if necessary, chopped

salt and pepper

>1 Preheat the oven to 200°C/400°F/Gas Mark 6. Melt the butter with the oil in a heavy-based saucepan with a lid, over a medium–high heat. Add the leeks and stir until well coated. Stir in salt and pepper to taste.

>2 Add a few gratings of nutmeg, then cover the leeks with a sheet of wet greaseproof paper and cover the pan. Reduce the heat to very low and leave the leeks to sweat for 5–7 minutes until very tender, but not brown. Stir in the chives, then taste and adjust the seasoning if necessary.

Serve immediately, while the crêpes are still hot.

>3 Put one crêpe on the work surface and put one eighth of the leeks on the crêpe, top with one eighth of the cheese.

>4 Fold the crêpe into a square parcel or simply roll it around the filling. Place the stuffed crêpe on a baking tray, then continue to fill and fold or roll the remaining crêpes. Bake in the preheated oven for 5 minutes, or until the crêpes are hot and the cheese starts to melt.

sweetcorn, chilli & tortilla gratin

serves 4–6

ingredients

groundnut oil, for greasing
and frying
6 corn cobs, with husks
2 green peppers
2–3 green chillies

6 corn tortillas, sliced into
2.5-cm/1-inch strips
225 g/8 oz vegetarian
Cheddar cheese, coarsely
grated

2 tbsp chopped fresh
coriander, to garnish

tomato sauce

8–10 tomatoes
1 onion, sliced into thick
rings
3 garlic cloves
sea salt and pepper

> **1** Preheat the oven to 190°C/375°F/ Gas Mark 5. Preheat the grill to high. Grease a 2-litre/3½-pint ovenproof dish.

> **2** Place the sweetcorn under the hot grill and cook, turning, for 10 minutes. Discard the husks. Slice off the kernels and reserve.

> **3** Place the green peppers and chillies under the hot grill and cook until blackened. Discard the skins and seeds. Roughly chop the flesh and reserve.

> **4** To make the tomato sauce, place the tomatoes, onion and garlic under the hot grill and cook until blackened. Remove the tomato stalks but not the skins. Transfer to a food processor and process to a chunky purée.

187

> **5** Heat 2 tablespoons of oil in a frying pan. Stir in the tomato mixture and simmer for 10 minutes, until thickened. Season with salt and pepper, then pour into a large bowl.

> **6** Heat 5 mm/¼ inch of oil in a large frying pan over a medium–high heat. Add the tortilla strips, in batches, and fry for 2–3 minutes, until crisp. Drain on kitchen paper. Stir into the tomato mixture, mixing well.

> **7** Arrange one third of the tortilla strips in the prepared dish. Sprinkle with half the green pepper mixture, half the corn and one third of the cheese. Season with salt and pepper.

> **8** Add another layer of tortilla strips, the remaining corn and green pepper mixture and half the remaining cheese. Season again, then add the rest of the tortilla strips and cheese. Bake in the preheated oven for 30 minutes, until golden.

Sprinkle with the chopped coriander and serve hot.

creamed morels on spinach & polenta croûtons

serves 4–6

ingredients

6 handfuls fresh morels
3 tbsp olive oil
4 shallots, finely chopped
2 garlic cloves, crushed
100 ml/3½ fl oz Marsala
200 ml/7 fl oz double cream
2 tbsp wholegrain mustard

1 small bunch fresh tarragon, finely chopped, plus extra to garnish
salt and pepper

polenta croûtons

1 litre/1¾ pints vegetable stock
250 g/9 oz quick-cook polenta
olive oil, for greasing
100 g/3½ oz freshly grated vegetarian Parmesan-style cheese

2 handfuls baby spinach, roughly torn
2 tsp coarsely cracked black peppercorns
100 g/3½ oz butter, softened
salt and pepper

>1 To make the croûtons, pour the stock into a large saucepan and bring to a rolling boil. Add the polenta in a steady stream, stirring quickly with a large balloon whisk. Cook according to the packet instructions. Lightly oil an oven dish.

>2 Use a wooden spoon to stir the cheese, spinach, peppercorns and half the butter into the polenta. Taste and adjust the seasoning, if necessary.

>3 Pour out the polenta mixture into the prepared dish, smooth with a palette knife and leave to cool. When the polenta has set, use a 10-cm/4-inch round pastry cutter to cut out the required number of rounds.

>4 Cut the morels in half and gently wash them, taking care to remove any traces of soil and grit. Dry gently with kitchen paper. Heat the oil in a saucepan over a medium heat, add the shallots and garlic and cook for 3–4 minutes, until soft.

> **5** Add the morels and cook, stirring constantly, for 2 minutes. Pour in the Marsala and bubble briefly; then add the cream, mustard and tarragon. Season to taste with salt and pepper. Keep warm.

> **6** Heat the remaining butter in a frying pan over a high heat, add the polenta croûtons and cook for 3–4 minutes on each side until crisp and golden.

Serve the croûtons immediately, heaped with the creamed morels and garnished with tarragon.

red cabbage stuffed with mushrooms, nuts & rice

serves 4–6

ingredients

50 g/1¾ oz butter
1 large red cabbage
juice of 2 lemons
3 tbsp olive oil
1 onion, chopped
150 g/5½ oz mushrooms,
  chopped

175 g/6 oz mixed nuts,
  chopped
3 garlic cloves, chopped
2 tbsp chopped fresh
  oregano
115 g/4 oz cooked
  Camargue red rice

300 ml/10 fl oz vegetable
  stock
sea salt and pepper

tomato sauce

8–10 tomatoes
1 onion, sliced into thick
  rings
3 garlic cloves
2 tbsp groundnut oil

>1 Preheat the oven to 180°C/350°F/ Gas Mark 4. Grease a 1-litre/1¾-pint round ovenproof dish with butter.

>2 Bring a saucepan of lightly salted water to the boil. Remove 8–10 cabbage leaves and plunge into the boiling water. Add half the lemon juice and boil for 4 minutes. Drain and pat dry. Shave off the thickest part of the stalk.

>3 Cut the remaining cabbage in half lengthways, reserving half for another recipe. Cut into quarters and discard the core. Shred the leaves.

>4 Heat the oil and half the butter in a large frying pan over a medium heat. Add the onion and fry for 5 minutes, until translucent.

> **5** Add the mushrooms, nuts, chopped cabbage, garlic, oregano, and salt and pepper to taste and cook for 5 minutes.

> **6** Stir in the rice, remaining lemon juice and half the stock and cook for a further 2 minutes.

> **7** Arrange the cabbage leaves around the edge and base of the prepared dish, leaving no gaps. Fill with the stuffing, pressing it in well. Dot with the remaining butter.

> **8** Fold over the tops of the leaves. Pour the remaining stock round the edge. Tightly cover with thick foil, and bake in the preheated oven for 45–50 minutes. Meanwhile, make the tomato sauce (see steps 4 and 5, pages 187-188).

Serve the cabbage in wedges,
accompanied by the tomato sauce.

197

fennel risotto with vodka

serves 4–5

ingredients

2 large fennel bulbs
2 tbsp vegetable oil
80 g/2¾ oz unsalted butter
1 large onion, finely
  chopped

350 g/12 oz risotto rice
150 ml/5 fl oz vodka or
  lemon-flavoured vodka
1.3 litres/2¼ pints hot
  vegetable stock

55 g/2 oz freshly grated
  vegetarian Parmesan-style
  cheese
5–6 tbsp lemon juice

> **1** Trim the fennel, reserving the fronds to garnish. Cut the bulbs in half lengthways, remove the V-shaped cores and roughly chop the flesh.

> **2** Heat the oil and half the butter in a large, heavy-based saucepan over a medium heat. Add the onion and fennel and cook for about 2 minutes, stirring frequently, until soft.

> **3** Add the rice and cook for about 2 minutes, stirring frequently, or until the rice is translucent and well coated.

> **4** Pour the vodka into the saucepan. It will bubble rapidly and evaporate almost immediately. Add a ladleful of the hot stock. Cook, stirring constantly, until all the stock has been absorbed.

>5 Continue stirring in the stock, about half a ladleful at a time, allowing each addition to be absorbed by the rice before adding the next. Cook for 20–25 minutes, or until all the liquid is absorbed and the rice is creamy.

>6 Stir in the remaining butter, the grated cheese and lemon juice. Remove from the heat, cover and leave to stand for 1 minute before serving.

Garnish with a few of the reserved fennel
fronds, and serve immediately.

sprouting broccoli with pine nuts & caper butter sauce

serves 4

ingredients

700 g/1 lb 9 oz purple
  sprouting broccoli
3 tbsp extra virgin olive oil
3 shallots, thinly sliced
2 large garlic cloves, thinly
  sliced

pinch of red chilli flakes
3 tbsp pine nuts
  toasted
55 g/2 oz butter
2 tbsp capers, drained
4 tbsp snipped chives

25 g/1 oz vegetarian
  Parmesan-style cheese,
  shaved into wafers
sea salt and pepper
cooked pasta shapes,
  to serve

>1 Cut off the broccoli florets and slice lengthways if thick. Slice the leaves and stems into 2-cm/¾-inch pieces. Steam for 2 minutes over a saucepan of boiling water, until barely soft. Remove from the heat. Reserve the cooking water.

>2 Heat the oil in a large frying pan over a medium–low heat. Add the shallots and fry for 5 minutes.

>3 Add the garlic and fry for 2–3 minutes, until just starting to colour.

>4 Increase the heat to medium and add the broccoli. Add the chilli flakes and season with salt and pepper. Add 3–4 tablespoons of the broccoli cooking water. Cook, stirring, for 4–6 minutes, until the broccoli is just tender and still bright green.

>5 Stir in the pine nuts and check the seasoning. Tip into a serving dish and keep warm.

>6 Heat a heavy-based frying pan. When it is very hot, add the butter. Sizzle until golden.

>7 Remove from the heat and stir in the capers and half the chives.

>8 Pour the sauce over the broccoli. Sprinkle with the cheese and the remaining chives.

Serve immediately with the pasta.

mixed nut roast with cranberry & red wine sauce

serves 4

ingredients

2 tbsp butter, plus extra
  for greasing
2 garlic cloves, chopped
1 large onion, chopped
50 g/1¾ oz pine nuts,
  toasted

75 g/2¾ oz hazelnuts,
  toasted
50 g/1¾ oz ground walnuts
50 g/1¾ oz ground cashew
  nuts
100 g/3½ oz wholemeal
  breadcrumbs

1 egg, lightly beaten
2 tbsp chopped fresh thyme
250 ml/9 fl oz vegetable
  stock
salt and pepper
sprigs of fresh thyme,
  to garnish

**cranberry & red wine
sauce**
175 g/6 oz fresh cranberries
100 g/3½ oz caster sugar
300 ml/10 fl oz red wine
1 cinnamon stick

>1 Preheat the oven to 180°C/350°F/ Gas Mark 4. Grease a 450-g/1-lb loaf tin and line it with greaseproof paper.

>2 Melt the butter in a saucepan over a medium heat. Add the garlic and onion and cook, stirring, for about 3 minutes. Remove the pan from the heat.

>3 Grind the pine nuts and hazelnuts in a mortar with a pestle.

>4 Stir into the pan with the walnuts and cashew nuts and add the breadcrumbs, egg, thyme, stock and seasoning.

> **5** Spoon the mixture into the loaf tin and level the surface. Cook in the centre of the preheated oven for 30 minutes or until cooked through and golden.

> **6** Insert a skewer into the centre of the loaf – it's cooked if the skewer comes out clean.

> **7** Halfway through the cooking time, make the sauce. Put all the ingredients into a saucepan and bring to the boil. Reduce the heat and simmer, stirring occasionally, for 15 minutes.

> **8** Remove the nut roast from the oven and turn out onto a serving platter.

Garnish the roast with sprigs of thyme and
serve with the cranberry and red wine sauce.

roast beetroot parcels with horseradish butter & polenta

serves 4

ingredients

olive oil, for greasing and tossing
8 small beetroots, peeled and halved
4 fresh thyme sprigs

4 tbsp grated fresh horseradish, or grated horseradish from a jar
125 g/4½ oz unsalted butter
sea salt flakes and pepper
rocket leaves, to serve

polenta

850 ml/1½ pints water
175 g/6 oz quick-cook polenta
1 tsp salt

> **1** To make the polenta, bring the water to the boil in a large saucepan. Slowly add the polenta and salt, stirring constantly. Simmer, stirring frequently, for 30–40 minutes, until the mixture comes away from the side of the pan.

> **2** Grease a small roasting tin. Tip the polenta into the tin, level the surface and leave to cool.

> **3** Preheat the oven to 190°C/375°F/Gas Mark 5. Toss the beetroots with enough oil to coat.

> **4** Place 4 beetroot halves and a thyme sprig on a square of thick foil. Season to taste. Wrap in a loose parcel, sealing the edges. Repeat with the remaining beetroots.

> **5** Roast in the preheated oven for about 1 hour or until just tender.

> **6** Meanwhile, mash the horseradish with the butter, ½ teaspoon of salt and ¼ teaspoon of pepper. Roll into a log using a piece of clingfilm and chill in the refrigerator.

> **7** Preheat the grill to high. Slice the polenta into four neat rectangles. Spread out in a grill pan, brush with oil and cook under a hot grill for 5 minutes. Turn and grill for a further 3 minutes, until crisp.

> **8** Arrange the polenta on serving plates. Place the beetroot and a slice of horseradish butter on top.

Add a handful of rocket to each plate and serve immediately.

chard & ricotta filo pie

serves 9

ingredients

900 g/2 lb rainbow chard
55 g/2 oz butter
2 leeks, sliced
2 garlic cloves, thinly
  sliced

3 tbsp chopped mixed
  fresh herbs, such as thyme,
  marjoram and flat-leaf
  parsley
400 g/14 oz ricotta cheese

55 g/2 oz freshly grated
  vegetarian Parmesan-style
  cheese
⅛ tsp freshly grated
  nutmeg

2 eggs, beaten
12 large sheets filo pastry
olive oil, for brushing
55 g/2 oz pine nuts
sea salt and pepper

> **1** Chop the chard stems into chunks. Slice the leaves into thin ribbons.

> **2** Heat the butter in a large frying pan over a medium heat. Add the leeks and chard stalks, cover and fry for 5–7 minutes, until soft.

> **3** Add the chard leaves, garlic and herbs. Cover and gently fry until the leaves are tender. Tip the vegetables into a colander and drain.

> **4** Beat together the ricotta cheese, Parmesan-style cheese, nutmeg and eggs in a large bowl. Mix in the drained vegetables. Season with salt and pepper.

>5 Preheat the oven to 190°C/375°F/Gas Mark 5. Place 1 sheet of filo pastry in a greased 23 x 30-cm/9 x 12-inch roasting tin, trimming to fit as necessary. Brush with oil and sprinkle with a few pine nuts. Add 5 more sheets, lightly brushing each one with oil and sprinkling with pine nuts.

>6 Pour in the filling and level the surface. Cover with 5 more sheets of filo pastry, brushing each sheet with oil and sprinkling with pine nuts. Add the final sheet and brush with oil.

>7 Using a sharp knife, cut through all the pastry and filling layers to make 7.5-cm/3-inch squares.

>8 Bake in the preheated oven for 35–40 minutes, until golden and crisp.

Cut into squares and serve hot or at room temperature.

kale & butter bean casserole with lime & chilli

serves 6

ingredients

350 g/12 oz butter beans, soaked overnight
1 tbsp cumin seeds
2 tsp dried oregano
3 tbsp groundnut oil
2 onions, chopped

2 garlic cloves, thinly sliced
1–3 fresh red or green chillies, deseeded and sliced
400 g/14 oz canned chopped tomatoes

450 ml/16 fl oz vegetable stock
175 g/6 oz shredded kale
5 tbsp chopped fresh coriander
juice of 1 lime

sea salt and pepper
2 avocados, cubed and tossed with lime juice, and red onion slivers, to garnish

> **1** Drain the beans, put them into a large saucepan and cover with water. Boil rapidly for 15 minutes, then reduce the heat and simmer for 30–45 minutes, until tender but not disintegrating. Drain and set aside.

> **2** Put the cumin seeds into a small dry frying pan over a medium heat and fry until fragrant. Add the oregano, fry for a few seconds, then immediately remove the mixture from the pan.

> **3** Lightly crush the mixture in a mortar with a pestle.

> **4** Heat the oil in a large, flameproof casserole over a medium heat. Add the onions and the spice and herb mixture. Fry for 5 minutes, until the chopped onions are translucent. Add the garlic and chillies and fry for a further 2 minutes.

>5 Stir in the tomatoes, beans and stock. Season with salt and pepper and bring to the boil. Reduce the heat, cover and simmer for 30 minutes, stirring occasionally.

>6 Increase the heat and stir in the kale. Simmer, uncovered, for 7 minutes, or until tender but still brightly coloured. Stir in the coriander and lime juice.

Ladle into soup plates, garnish with the avocado and red onion and serve immediately.

Index